History's Mysteries

Bog Mummies
WHERE DID THEY COME FROM?

MEGAN COOLEY PETERSON

BLACK
RABBIT
BOOKS

Bolt is published by Black Rabbit Books
P.O. Box 3263, Mankato, Minnesota, 56002.
www.blackrabbitbooks.com
Copyright © 2019 Black Rabbit Books

Jennifer Besel, editor; Grant Gould, designer;
Omay Ayres, photo researcher

Library of Congress Cataloging-in-Publication Data
Names: Peterson, Megan Cooley, author.
Title: Bog mummies : where did they come from? / by Megan Cooley
Peterson.
Description: Mankato, Minnesota : Black Rabbit Books, 2019. | Series: Bolt.
History's mysteries | Includes bibliographical references and index. |
Audience: Age 8-12. | Audience: Grade 4 to 6.
Identifiers: LCCN 2017035851 (print) | LCCN 2017040033 (ebook) |
ISBN 9781680725230 (ebook) | ISBN 9781680724073 (library binding) |
ISBN 9781680727012 (paperback)
Subjects: LCSH: Bog bodies—Juvenile literature.
Classification: LCC GN744 (ebook) | LCC GN744 .P48 2019 (print) |
DDC 393/.3—dc23
LC record available at https://lccn.loc.gov/2017035851

Printed in China. 3/18

Image Credits

Alamy: SOTK2011, 20 (t); com-
mons.wikimedia.org: 15EmmettTill, 1;
Bullenwächter, Cover (face), 18–19, 21, 29
(body); Elgaard, 16 (t); Flickr, Mark Healey, 9
(b), Gourami Watcher, 15 (b); NearEMPTiness, 20
(b); Sven Rosborn, 8, 12 (t); Unknown, 25; Dream-
stime: Designua, 16–17 (b); iStock: unkas_photo, 24;
Newscom: Christian Kober/robertharding, 4–5; nps.
gov: National Parks Service, 22; Science Source: Carlos
Muñoz-Yagüe, 3, 6, 9 (t), 26, 31, 32; Shutterstock: az-
botaa, 23; Brocreative, 15 (t); Maria Isaeva, Cover, 29
(magnifying glass); Oleg Golovnev, 29 (paper)
Every effort has been made to contact copyright
holders for material reproduced in this book.
Any omissions will be rectified in subse-
quent printings if notice is given to
the publisher.

CONTENTS

CHAPTER 1

What Lies

It was 1950. A family near Tollund, Denmark, cut **peat** in a **bog**. Suddenly, the family members were staring at a dead body. They called police. They feared the man had recently been murdered.

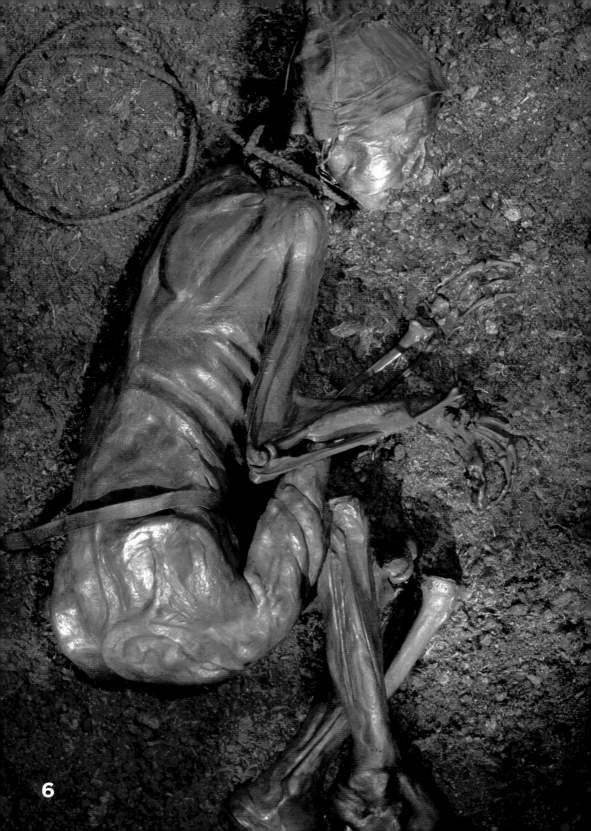

Surprising Discovery

Police and scientists arrived in the bog. They soon realized what an important discovery this was. The family had found a bog mummy. The body was more than 2,000 years old!

Bog mummies are one of history's great mysteries. Why are bodies in bogs? Did they fall in? Or were they put there on purpose?

The mummy the family found is called Tollund Man.

CHAPTER 2

FINDING Bog Mummies

People have found bog mummies since the 1700s. These strange bodies are found in peat bogs. **Acid** in the bogs' plants keep the bodies from breaking down. It turns them into mummies.

Well Preserved

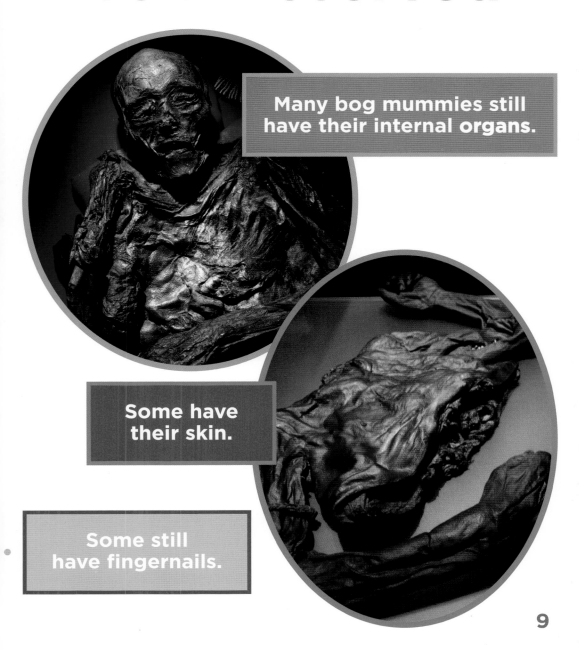

Many bog mummies still have their internal organs.

Some have their skin.

Some still have fingernails.

SOME PLACES WHERE BOG MUMMIES HAVE BEEN DISCOVERED

IRELAND

ENGLAND

UNITED STATES

THE NETHERLANDS

DENMARK

GERMANY

People have found more than 1,000 bog mummies in Europe.

Bog Mummies in Europe

Mummies found in Europe are very old. Most were buried nearly 3,000 years ago. Did **ancient** people know the bogs would **preserve** the bodies? No one knows for sure. There are no written records from that time.

= 100 mummies

Bog Mummies in Florida

In 1982, **archaeologists** dug up mummies in Florida. The mummies no longer had skin. But many still had brains. These bog mummies were buried about 8,000 years ago. Scientists have found more than 160 bodies there.

A construction worker discovered the first Florida mummy. The worker was clearing the area for new houses.

Forming a Peat Bog

1
Peat bogs begin as ponds or lakes. • • • • • • •►

2
Plants grow around the lake. They sink to the lake bottom when they die. • • • •

3
After hundreds of years, the dead plants fill the lake. The plants are called peat. • • • • • • • • • •

CHAPTER 3

INVESTIGATING
Bog Mummies

So how did bodies end up in the bogs? That's what scientists want to find out. Many European bog mummies appear to have been killed. Tollund Man had a leather rope around his neck. Others had stab wounds or broken bones.

Religious Sacrifices?

The European mummies also often had jewelry, weapons, and armor. Some scientists think ancient people believed bogs were gates to the **afterlife**. Maybe they thought the dead needed these items.

Other scientists think the people were criminals. They might have been buried in the bogs as punishments.

19

HOW TO MAKE A BOG MUMMY

Step 1

A body is put into a bog.

Step 2

Acid in the moss turns skin into leather.

Step 3

Layers of plants seal the body in the bog. A lack of oxygen keeps the body from rotting.

Buried with Care?

The bog mummies in Florida tell a
different story. Many appeared to be
buried with care. One mummy died as
a young girl. She was buried with toys,
including a turtle's shell. • • • • •

No Answers

Many Florida mummies were found lying on their left sides. Their faces pointed north. Historians aren't sure why. Some guess it may have been for religious reasons.

Scientists found more than 3,000 elderberry seeds in one mummy's stomach. She might have eaten them to fight an **infection**.

CHAPTER 4

You DECIDE

Scientists have many questions about bog mummies. Were they carefully laid to rest? Or did they meet violent ends? Researchers continue to look for clues. Maybe one day people will have answers to this mystery.

Asking Questions to Solve the Mystery

Researchers ask questions to solve history's mysteries. You can too!

 Who were the people buried in the bogs?

 What do the mummies' burials tell you about them?

 When were the bodies put in the bogs?

 Where are the most bog mummies found?

WHY?

Why are bodies buried in the peat?

HOW?

How did the bog mummies form?

What other questions do you have?

GLOSSARY

acid (AHS-id)—a chemical substance that can dissolve some things

afterlife (AHF-tur-liyf)—a life after death

ancient (AYN-shunt)—from a long time ago

archaeologist (ahr-kee-OL-uh-jist)— someone who studies bones, tools, and lives of ancient people

bog (BOG)—a type of wetland that includes wet, spongy ground and pools of muddy water

infection (in-FEK-shun)—a disease caused by germs that enter the body

organ (OHR-guhn)—a bodily structure consisting of cells and tissues that performs a specific function

peat (PEET)—a material that is the remains of plants partly decayed in water; people used to burn peat for fuel.

preserve (pree-ZURV)—to keep alive, intact, or free from decay

BOOKS

Malam, John. *Mummies.* 100 Facts You Should Know. New York: Gareth Stevens Publishing, 2015.

Merwin, E. *Mummy Tombs.* Tiptoe into Scary Places. New York: Bearport Publishing Company, Inc., 2018.

Small, Cathleen. *Mummies.* Creatures of Fantasy. New York: Cavendish Square Publishing, 2017.

WEBSITES

Bodies of the Bogs
archive.archaeology.org/online/features/bog

Tales from the Bog
ngm.nationalgeographic.com/2007/09/bog-bodies/bog-bodies-text.html

The Perfect Corpse
www.pbs.org/wgbh/nova/bog/iron-nf.html

INDEX